S0-AZF-834

HERO JOURNALS

Julius Caesar

Nick Hunter

Chicago, Illinois

Edited by Adam Miller, Charlotte Guillain,
and Claire Throp
Designed by Richard Parker and
Ken Vail Graphic Design
Original illustrations © Capstone Global
Library Ltd 2014
Illustrated by Mat Edwards (Advocate Art)
Picture research Tracy Cummins
Production by Victoria Fitzgerald
Originated by Capstone Global Library Ltd
Printed and bound in China by Leo
Paper Products Ltd

17 16 15 14 13
10 9 8 7 6 5 4 3 2 1

**Library of Congress Cataloging-in-Publication
Data**
Hunter, Nick.
Julius Caesar / Nick Hunter.
p. cm.—(Hero journals)
Includes bibliographical references and index.
ISBN 978-1-4109-5356-8 (hb)—ISBN 978-1-4109-
5363-6 (pb) 1. Caesar, Julius—Juvenile literature.
2. Heads of state—Rome—Biography—Juvenile
literature. 3. Generals—Rome—Biography—
Juvenile literature. 4. Rome—History—Republic,
265-30 B.C.—Juvenile literature. I. Title.
DG261.H86 2014
937'.05092—dc23   2012043471

Acknowledgments
We would like to thank the following for
permission to reproduce photographs: Art
Resource, NY pp. 12 (© The Trustees of the British
Museum), 16 (Gianni Dagli Orti/The Art Archive),
27 (bpk, Berlin), 29 (Alfredo Dagli Orti/The Art
Archive), 30–31 (NGS Image Collection/The Art
Archive), 37 (Gianni Dagli Orti/The Art Archive);
The Bridgeman Art Library pp. 9 (Louvre, Paris,
France), 26 (Giraudon); Corbis pp. 11 (© National
Geographic Society), 19 (© Bettmann), 21
(© Bettmann); Getty Images pp. 6 (Simeone
Huber), 7 (Hulton Archive), 20 (Walter Bibikow),
25 (Robert Harding World Imagery), 32 (De
Agostini Picture Library), 35 (DEA/G. Nimatallah);
Shutterstock pp. 5 (PerseoMedusa), 15 (Yiannis
Papadimitriou), 23 (Filip Fuxa), 39 (PerseoMedusa);
Superstock pp. 14, 36 (Hoberman Collection).
Design features reproduced with permission of
Shutterstock (R-studio, Pavel K, Picsfive, karawan).

Cover photograph of a sculpture depicting
Roman Emperor Julius Caesar reproduced
with permission of Getty Images (Nelson
Almeida/AFP).

Every effort has been made to contact copyright
holders of material reproduced in this book. Any
omissions will be rectified in subsequent printings
if notice is given to the publisher.

All the Internet addresses (URLs) given in this
book were valid at the time of going to press.
However, due to the dynamic nature of the
Internet, some addresses may have changed,
or sites may have changed or ceased to exist
since publication. While the author and publisher
regret any inconvenience this may cause readers,
no responsibility for any such changes can be
accepted by either the author or the publisher.

Contents

Who Is Julius Caesar?

Hi, I'm Julius, but most people call me Caesar. I don't mean to be bigheaded, but it is hard to be humble when you're one of the greatest generals who ever lived. If you haven't heard of me, you must know about the mighty Roman Empire that stretched from Africa to Britain. That huge empire would not have existed without my amazing conquests in Gaul (modern France).

Being one of history's greatest generals would be enough for most people, but I also wanted to be a ruler, or even the greatest Roman of them all. I set out to change Rome and create an empire that would last for hundreds of years.

Gaul

Gaul was the name for the area north and west of Rome. It included what is now northern Italy, France, Belgium, and parts of Germany.

Making enemies

Given how much I did for them, you'd think that the Romans would appreciate me a little more. Of course, they didn't. Powerful people in Rome didn't always like my methods or how popular I was with the ordinary people. They were always plotting to get rid of me. So what if I broke a few rules? If you don't want to get stepped on, don't stand in the way!

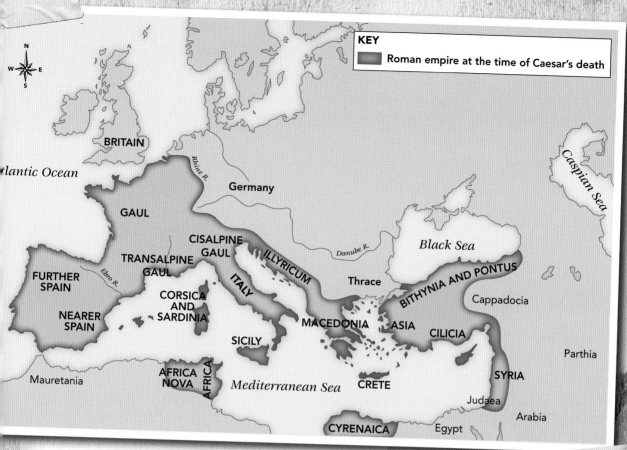

KEY

Roman empire at the time of Caesar's death

Atlantic Ocean

BRITAIN

Rhine R.

Germany

GAUL

CISALPINE GAUL

TRANSALPINE GAUL

Ebro R.

ILLYRICUM

Danube R.

Black Sea

Caspian Sea

FURTHER SPAIN

ITALY

Thrace

BITHYNIA AND PONTUS

Cappadocia

NEARER SPAIN

CORSICA AND SARDINIA

MACEDONIA

ASIA

CILICIA

Parthia

SICILY

CRETE

SYRIA

Mauretania

AFRICA NOVA

AFRICA

Mediterranean Sea

Judaea

Arabia

CYRENAICA

Egypt

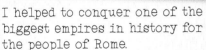

I helped to conquer one of the biggest empires in history for the people of Rome.

The Romans love to put up statues of their heroes, and there were plenty of me.

Document it!

Julius Caesar lived more than 2,000 years ago. We know about his life from what others wrote about him, and from what he wrote about his own life and military campaigns. You can write your own journal to record what happens in your life.

5

Birth of a Genius: My Early Years

I was born in Rome on July 12 in the year 100 BCE. In Roman years, that was the year 653 after the founding of Rome. My family had a proud history, and we used to say we were descended from kings and even a goddess. I was called Gaius Julius Caesar, just like my father.

Sadly, although the family was ancient and noble, we weren't very rich compared to the greedy people who ruled Rome. Money and power went together in the Roman Republic, and we didn't have much of either.

Ancient Rome was the greatest city in the world for an ambitious young man to grow up in.

Life was good for the noble families of Rome. Slaves did all the hard work for us.

Taking sides

But it wasn't all bad. People in Rome were getting sick of the same old faces running the show. When I was a child, different leaders were battling for power in Rome, and there were opportunities for ambitious young men if you supported the right side. Unfortunately, my family had a habit of supporting the wrong side.

Republic on the rise

By 100 BCE, Rome had defeated a challenge from the rival city of Carthage. Rome now ruled over many lands around the Mediterranean Sea. Closer to home, many Romans were unhappy with the way their city was being run. Rome was a republic with no king, and just a few powerful and wealthy families had control over the whole city.

Getting an education

Of course, I had a bit of growing up to do before I would worry about the world of politics. Children of noble families did not go to school. We were normally taught at home by our parents or a tutor. My tutor was a former slave named Marcus Antonius Gnipho. He taught me to read and write in Latin (the Roman language) and ancient Greek. Speaking in public was also important for anyone like me who wanted a political career.

Noble Romans taught their sons "reading and writing, the law, physical education, and all sorts of outdoor skills such as throwing the javelin, fighting in armor, riding, boxing, swimming, and how to stand up to heat and cold."

The writer Plutarch

Like all noble Romans, I used to watch my father at work. For a time, he was governor in an eastern province called Asia Minor, so we lived away from Rome. But when I was just 16 years old, my father died suddenly. I was very close to my mother, Aurelia, and she was a very tough woman. But the world of political power in Rome was only open to men...I would have to fend for myself.

Document it!

We know very little about Caesar's childhood and education. However, writing about what happens at school and at home can be a lot of fun, and it can be interesting to read what you wrote when you're a little older and see how you have changed. Think about whether you are writing for yourself or for other people to read it, since this will affect what you write about.

This marble carving shows scenes from the life of a wealthy boy, including riding in a chariot pulled by a goat.

Bad start

I was determined to be a success in Roman politics, but it was a difficult time to grow up. Powerful men were fighting to lead Rome. If you were on the wrong side, you could find yourself at the bottom of the Tiber River.

Marriage mishap

I married Cornelia in 84 BCE, when I was just a teenager. She was rich and had great political connections. But there was a problem. In 82 BCE, Lucius Cornelius Sulla took power. Cornelia's father and my uncle had fought against Sulla for control of Rome. When Sulla took over, we were definitely not flavor of the month.

When Sulla came to power, my political career was very nearly ended before it had even begun. He tried to embarrass me by ordering me to leave Cornelia to show my loyalty to him. No one tells Caesar what to do!

I wasn't about to give in to Sulla, but I did have to get out of Rome for a while. Things were getting a bit complicated. Even worse, the dictator took all our money!

Lucius Cornelius Sulla

Sulla was Rome's first dictator, from 82 to 79 BCE. He carried out much-needed reforms in Rome, but he was ruthless in dealing with his enemies. Caesar was probably saved because he was so young and no threat to the dictator.

> *"Bear in mind that the man you are so eager to save will one day deal the death blow to the cause of the aristocracy."*

Sulla warns the followers who urged him to spare Caesar's life

The Roman army parades prisoners through the streets of Rome. Joining the army was a great way to make your name.

Making My Mark

While Sulla was murdering his enemies in Rome, I stayed out of the way. I joined the army. I traveled the known world and defeated any barbarians who dared to get in my way. This was a lot of fun, but I was really just waiting until the coast was clear in Rome.

Pirates had roamed the Mediterranean Sea for hundreds of years. This Greek vase shows pirates attacking a merchant ship.

While I was away from Rome, there was always the risk of falling into the hands of pirates. That's just what happened when I was journeying to the Greek island of Rhodes.

Pirates in peril

But these scruffy and hopeless pirates were no match for me, the soon-to-be-mighty Caesar. They were planning to ask for a very low ransom to release me — far less than I was worth. I told them to ask for more money. I assured them I would personally see that they were captured and killed, so they might as well get as much as they could. If they thought I was worth a big ransom, they would be less likely to kill me.

After they released me, I found some ships of my own and caught those puny pirates. I kindly asked for their throats to be cut before they were crucified. This made their deaths a little less painful and lingering. After all, I'm not one to hold a grudge.

Pirates in the Mediterranean

Piracy was a big problem for Rome. Whole communities in Cyprus, Crete, and other islands lived off piracy, often by capturing and selling slaves. In 67 BCE, Rome decided that enough was enough, and a fleet of 500 ships, 120,000 foot soldiers, and 5,000 cavalry was sent to root out the pirates.

Into battle

Sulla died in 78 BCE, and I was then free to launch my political career in Rome. But there were still plenty of battles to be fought. Mithradates ruled Pontus on the coast of the Black Sea. He had been causing trouble for years. To become king, he had imprisoned his mother, killed his brother, and married his sister. Then, in 74 BCE, he invaded the Roman province of Asia Minor. I led an army against him.

Now that I was a war hero, ordinary people in Rome were starting to hear about me. Events like Spartacus's slave revolt of 73 BCE did not make people feel safe, and they were looking for tough leaders. Sounds like a job for Caesar?

I never had much time for making speeches in the Senate. I preferred action, and this landed me in plenty of trouble.

Spartacus

Spartacus was a former slave. His revolt started in a breakout from a gladiator school. The untrained but ferocious slave army won many battles before the Roman army finally crushed them. Spartacus and 6,000 followers were crucified by the merciless Romans.

I got the job of quaestor in 68 BCE. But without great riches or political connections, I had to make my name as a "man of the people." This served me well over the years.

The political ladder

Roman politicians could be elected to a number of different political roles. Quaestors worked in the law courts and were the lowest rung of the ladder. Aediles had to pay for public festivals and for repairing the streets. Praetors were the senior judges. At the top were the two consuls, who were the rulers of the Roman Republic. Consuls only ruled for one year at a time, and there were two of them, so neither had too much power.

Alexander the Great was one of my heroes. By the age of 30, Alexander was ruler of a great empire. When I was 30, I was still a junior magistrate in Rome.

Celebrity Caesar

In 68 BCE, everything seemed to be set for my glorious career. The biggest cloud was the death of my wife Cornelia, mother of our daughter, Julia. But every cloud has a silver lining, so I showed my grief by organizing an expensive public funeral, which got people talking about me again. Then I married Pompeia, a cousin of the great general Pompey. He would be both a friend and enemy over the years.

Men and women

Ancient Rome was a man's world. The worlds of business, politics, and the Roman army were closed to women. Women were usually in charge of the household and family, which could be a big job in the largest houses, with many slaves to organize. There were still powerful women in Rome, but their influence was usually behind the scenes.

Being popular with the people was expensive. When I was elected aedile in 65 BCE, people expected me to throw lavish parties and gladiator shows, even if I had to borrow the money to pay for them.

Debt and divorce

As if my growing debts weren't enough to deal with, I was accused of being mixed up in a plot against the consuls. That was bad enough, but then Pompeia got involved in a scandal around a women-only festival. I told everyone she was innocent, but I divorced her anyway. With all these problems piling up, 62 BCE seemed like a good time to lie low in distant Spain.

"Caesar's wife must be above suspicion."

Caesar explains why he divorced his wife, even though he said she'd done nothing wrong

17

Power and Riches

I wasn't on vacation in Spain. I was the governor, and that meant two things: cash and conquests.

Some people in Spain were not happy with Roman rule. They were even less happy when I'd finished restoring order. My armies plundered towns and silver mines. My soldiers were happy, and I could pay my debts. Now those grumpy old senators in Rome would have to listen to me. It was high time that Caesar got the top job back in Rome — consul!

My Spanish silver helped me to get elected as consul in 59 BCE. My enemies tried to stop it and made sure a fool named Bibulus was the other consul. He did everything he could to get in my way. In the end, I ignored him and did whatever I chose. People in Rome joked that there were two consuls: Julius and Caesar. If only!

Power of three

I could get my own way because I'd made a deal with two other important Romans. Pompous Pompey was Rome's greatest general (for now), and moneybags Crassus could buy anything or anyone he wanted. They called us the First Triumvirate, and we were unstoppable. Pompey married my daughter Julia to seal the deal.

Marcus Licinius Crassus

Crassus was the richest man in Rome. He had made a lot of money when Sulla was in charge, and bought influence by lending money to ambitious but poor senators like Caesar. He could also be a brutal general. When his army lost a battle to Spartacus' slave revolt, he selected 1 out of every 10 soldiers to be executed as a punishment.

By 59 BCE, I'd made it to the top job in Rome. But the consulship only lasted a year. What would I do next?

Caesar in charge

Rome's consuls have to be nice to everyone and follow the rules. But I never liked being told what to do, and a lot of Rome's top people would love to have seen me fail.

The sneaky Roman senators tried to put me in charge of forests and cattle tracks after my time as consul finished. Clearly, I would never allow that to happen. No one could say no to Caesar, Pompey, and Crassus. Instead, I opted to take over as governor of Cisalpine Gaul (now northern Italy) and Illyricum (modern Croatia, Bosnia, and Albania). I soon added the rest of Gaul across the Alps to my realm.

I now had my own provinces to rule and armies to command. Away from the squabbles and the boring speeches of Rome, I could get on with bringing Roman civilization to people, whether they wanted it or not.

My armies marched to the furthest corners of the empire on smooth Roman roads. But all the roads led back to Rome in the end.

Making plans

The scenery was nice, but I wasn't really interested in that. I had my eyes on the barbarian tribes in northern and western Gaul. It was time to do a bit of empire-building, just like my hero, Alexander the Great.

Calpurnia was my second-biggest fan—after myself, of course!

Calpurnia

Calpurnia married Caesar in 59 BCE to seal an alliance between Caesar and her father, Lucius Calpunius Piso Caesoninus. When they married, Calpurnia was a teenager and Caesar was almost 40 years old. Calpurnia was loyal to Caesar until his death, despite rumors of Caesar's affairs with other women, including the Egyptian queen Cleopatra. Calpurnia was said to have dreamed about Caesar's death and warned him in advance.

Conquest

Winning great victories in Gaul would show everyone what a brilliant general I was. Even if the senators still complained about me breaking a few little rules here and there, all the Roman people really care about is glory and conquests.

Going for Gaul

Gaul was made up of hundreds of different tribes. At first, I was just doing my job and protecting the borders of Rome from tribes of Helvetians and Germans to the north. But soon I decided that these barbarians in Gaul needed to be taught a lesson. They were brave but lacked Roman efficiency. It wasn't pretty, for the Gauls at least. I stormed 800 towns, defeated 300 tribes, and claimed huge new lands for the glory of Rome, and, most of all, for the glory of Julius Caesar!

My campaigns in Gaul lasted from 58 to 50 BCE.

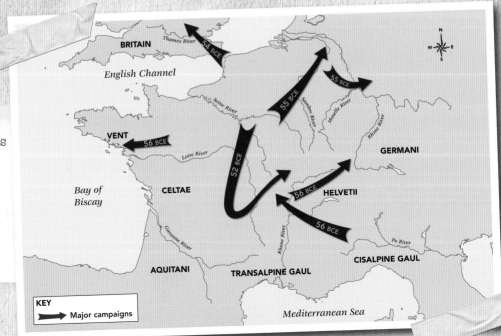

Caesar's legions

Caesar went to be governor of Cisalpine Gaul, with four legions of soldiers. He raised and trained several more and returned to Rome in 49 BCE with 11 legions. A legion was made up of around 4,500 foot soldiers. It did not include soldiers on horseback, and the Gauls probably had the edge in cavalry. But the highly trained, tough, and disciplined legions were the backbone of the Roman army and were almost always stronger than their enemies in Caesar's time.

"On the march he headed his army, sometimes on horseback but more often on foot...He covered great distances with incredible speed...swimming the rivers that barred his path or crossing them on inflated skins and very often arriving before the messengers sent to announce his coming."

Roman writer Suetonius describes Caesar's amazing energy

Gaul stayed under Roman rule for hundreds of years. We left them some amazing Roman buildings, such as this aqueduct.

Breaking the rules

Okay, maybe sometimes I went too far. The Usipetes and the Tencteri tribes from Germany were tough fighters and hard to beat. But many people back in Rome thought I had been too brutal by killing women and children in addition to their warriors. They threatened to hand me over to the Germans. What's wrong with these people? War is dirty, and you can't always play by the rules.

Brutish Britons

I also went too far north in 55 and 54 BCE. The Gauls were barbarians, but the Britons (see illustration below) made them look like civilized Romans. I should have known it would be a waste of time when they all appeared painted blue. Their towns were little more than mud huts, without a bathhouse in sight. But worst of all was the weather. My cavalry got blown back to Gaul by a storm before they even managed to reach the rotten country. Lucky them! People back home were impressed that I'd reached the ends of the Earth, but I wasn't going to spend any more effort invading a hopeless place like Britain.

Ancient Britain

Caesar was not impressed by the Britons. Many Romans were disappointed that this mysterious land did not contain mountains of gold and silver. The British tribes were not quite as primitive as the Romans thought. They traded with each other and across Europe. They were also skilled craft workers. Caesar decided that Britain was not worth invading, and the Romans did not return for almost 100 years.

The people of Britain built fortresses on tops of hills to protect themselves.

Trouble in Gaul

The Gauls were determined people who kept coming back for more. Vercingetorix, in particular, was a real test to my power. In 52 BCE, he started a revolt. For once, the Gaulish tribes were united, and he was supported by around 1,000 of them.

This Gaul was a true warrior. Don't tell anyone in Rome, but he even beat me in one battle. My soldiers had to be at their best to defeat him. We finally defeated the Gauls at the siege of Alesia. Vercingetorix was inside this stronghold, so we also had to defeat the large army coming to rescue him.

Vercingetorix put up a good fight, but eventually he had to lay down his weapons.

Vercingetorix was not the only Gaul who didn't realize how lucky he was to be part of the Roman Empire. I had to be tough with some of the survivors. Some people thought cutting off their hands was too much, but these people are not civilized like us Romans. Extreme violence is the only way to control them.

The siege of Alesia was one of my greatest victories.

Document it!

Caesar wrote a detailed history of his successes in Gaul, partly to impress people back in Rome. What would you write about your own successes, or what are your ambitions for the future? What words would you use to describe your greatest moments?

Vercingetorix

Vercingetorix was one of the few generals to win a victory against Caesar's forces. His success came from small-scale attacks on the Romans rather than meeting them in open battle. Finally, he surrendered at the siege of Alesia and was paraded through the streets of Rome as a prisoner before being executed.

Crossing the Rubicon

After my victories in Gaul, I was massively popular with the ordinary people back in Rome. Pompey had been Rome's greatest general before me, and he wasn't pleased. Moneybags Crassus wanted some glory, too. He led an army to Parthia in the east and got himself killed.

Tough choices

Even as the people's favorite, I needed some help in Rome. Pompey and I still worked together, but it was getting harder. In 50 BCE, the Senate asked me to hand over my legions in Gaul to a new governor. Despite all the new lands I'd won for Rome, they wanted me to stand trial for war crimes. They left me no choice.

In January 49 BCE, when I was 50 years old, I marched my army across the Rubicon River. This meant I was invading the Roman heartland. Rome could never allow me to get away with it, and I couldn't turn back. This was war.

Pompey the Great (Gnaeus Pompeius Magnus)

Pompey's victories in Africa, Spain, and Syria made him famous as a young man. He married Caesar's daughter to seal their alliance, but Julia died in 54 BCE. As Caesar became more successful, Pompey looked for other allies in Rome. They became bitter enemies.

Pompey wanted to keep power for himself. In the end, the Roman Empire was not big enough for both of us.

Staying one step ahead

Caesar had made too many enemies and broken too many rules to become a private citizen. As long as he was a senior official, such as a governor or a consul, he could not face a trial for his crimes. This was why Caesar needed allies like Pompey and Crassus to protect him while he was away from Rome.

Civil war

No one wanted civil war. Romans would be killing Romans instead of conquering the rest of the world. Pompey had been a good general in his time, but he couldn't accept that I was better. If Pompey and the rest of the senators thought I was going to back down, they were in for a shock.

The war was closely fought. Pompey had the power of Rome on his side, while I was the rebel whom they wanted to defeat. I quickly took Italy, but there was a lot of empire to fight over. Pompey won a couple of skirmishes in Greece. On August 9, 48 BCE, we faced each other in a "do or die" battle at Pharsalus in Greece. I won a great victory. Pompey fled to Egypt, and I set off after him to finish the job.

Mark Antony

Mark Antony was one of Caesar's biggest supporters. He fought alongside Caesar in Gaul, and Caesar made sure Antony was elected to several key jobs where he could help his cause. After Caesar's death, Antony started a famous love affair with the Egyptian queen Cleopatra. This affair led to him being forced from power in the Roman Empire and to his own death.

"It was only recently that Pompey had come to fear Caesar. Up till this time he had despised him. It was through his influence, he thought, that Caesar had grown great, and it would be just as easy to put him down as it had been to raise him up."

The historian Plutarch describes the jealousy and mistrust between Pompey and Caesar

As the civil war was fought across the Mediterranean Sea, war galleys (ships) like these were important.

Head start in Egypt

I must say I've had better-looking presents. But I was still pleased when I was given Pompey's severed head on my arrival in Egypt. The surprises didn't end there. I was brought a rolled up rug as a gift. Inside was the Egyptian queen Cleopatra. I was so enchanted with Cleopatra that I brought her back to Rome with me. The stuffy old Romans complained bitterly about "the Egyptian woman."

Cleopatra was a good politician. She knew she needed my help to succeed as queen of Egypt.

Egypt was a great place to spend time. It had been ruled by kings called pharaohs for thousands of years. The system seemed to work, and I don't know why the Romans were so set against the idea of kings, especially when there was one obvious candidate for the job!

Loose ends

There were still battles to be won. I had to fight Cleopatra's brother to help her gain power in Egypt, and then I had to tackle another rebellion in Asia. Finally, I defeated the remains of Pompey's allies at Thapsus in North Africa in 46 BCE. I was so pleased when the battle was won. Now I could start sorting out Rome.

I arrived in Alexandria in Egypt in 48 BCE.

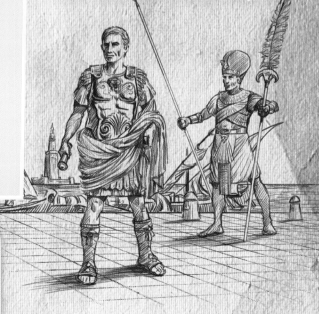

Cleopatra

Cleopatra had been named joint ruler of Egypt after her father died. But her brother Ptolemy had seized the throne, and Cleopatra needed Caesar's help to defeat him. After Caesar's death, Cleopatra ruled Egypt with her son Caesarion. Cleopatra claimed Caesar was Caesarion's father. Egypt became a province of the Roman Empire in 30 BCE.

"Veni. Vidi. Vici." ("I came. I saw. I conquered.")

Caesar uttered these famous words after a quick victory over a rebellion in Asia

Taking Charge

At last, in 46 BCE, I was on top of the world. I celebrated my victories with a great procession through the streets and one of the biggest parties Rome had ever seen. We celebrated like only Romans can, with plenty of blood and guts in the gladiator shows.

> *"A combat of gladiators and stage plays in every ward all over the city...as well as [chariot] races in the circus, athletic contests, and a sham [pretend] sea-fight."*
>
> Suetonius describes the celebrations as Caesar returned to Rome in triumph

Afterward, there was some serious work to be done. I was the dictator of Rome and could do whatever I wanted. Thanks to me, and a few others, Rome was now the capital of a huge empire stretching far beyond the shores of the Mediterranean Sea. But it could no longer be ruled in the same way as before. We needed more senators and officials.

Bread and circuses

Of course, the people in the Senate who'd hated me all along didn't like my changes, but there was nothing they could do about it. Ordinary Romans were happy as long as they got plenty of food and entertainment.

Republic vs. king

The Roman Republic had been formed when Romans overthrew their king in 509 BCE. The Republic was governed by magistrates such as the consuls who were elected for fixed periods from the Senate and other public bodies. The whole system was designed to make sure that no one person had too much power. Caesar's ambition to be dictator went against hundreds of years of history.

Marcus Junius Brutus was one of the most honest men in the Senate. He did a good job for me, but he didn't like the idea of a king of Rome.

Dictator of Rome

I must say things are going pretty well now. I've been voted dictator of Rome for the rest of my life. Mark Antony even offered me a crown so that I could be king. But I turned it down, because it would have really upset the senators who would love to get rid of me.

There's a ridiculous rumor of a plot against me. A foolish soothsayer told me to "beware the Ides of March." Why should I be afraid of the feast day of Mars?

The Ides of March

Well, the day has come, and I'm still here. Dear Calpurnia tried to persuade me not to go to the Senate today. But there's really nothing to worry about. No one can stop me now — I'm untouchable!

Some senators thought I was getting much too powerful when my head started appearing on Roman coins.

Assassination

On March 15, 44 BCE, Julius Caesar was murdered on the steps of the Senate house by a group of 60 men led by Marcus Junius Brutus. They hated the fact that Caesar was the sole leader of Rome. But Rome did not go back to being the republic the assassins longed for. After a bloody civil war, Rome was ruled by Caesar's descendants as emperors.

The killing of Caesar plunged
Rome into years of civil war.

Octavian
(Gaius Julius Caesar Octavianus)

Octavian was Caesar's great nephew, but he became his adopted successor. He was just 18 years old when Caesar was murdered. After defeating Brutus and the other plotters, Octavian ruled Italy and the western empire while Mark Antony ruled in the east. In 31 BCE, Octavian defeated Mark Antony to become the master of Rome. He became the first emperor, called *Augustus* (which means "majestic" in Latin), in 27 BCE.

Caesar in History

When Caesar died, Romans reported that the skies above Rome were dark for seven days and a comet appeared in the sky. His supporters believed this was Caesar's soul going to join the gods. Caesar was one of the greatest figures in history, but he divided opinions in Rome like no one else.

Caesar's conquests built the lands of Rome into one of the biggest and most powerful empires in history. Even the Romans who hated him had to admit his brilliance. He inspired fierce loyalty in his armies and among the ordinary people of Rome.

Flawed genius

But Caesar was also boastful and ambitious. He wanted power and didn't care how he got it. He was brutal to his enemies and broke rules of war.

Over the centuries, the name *Caesar* has come to mean another word for a great and powerful leader. Despite his many flaws, the name of Gaius Julius Caesar echoes through history.

How do we know about Caesar?

We know a lot about Caesar's life and career from his own writings on the wars in Gaul and the civil war. Friends and enemies also wrote about Caesar. We need to remember that many of these sources can be biased. Caesar's writings show his own point of view, while his critics wanted to make the dictator look as bad as possible. Statues show what he looked like. But we know less about his family life and childhood.

We know what
Caesar looked
like from
statues created
by the Romans.

"His character was a mix of genius, method, memory,
culture, thoroughness, intellect, and industry."

Roman senator Cicero was no fan of Caesar, but had to admit his greatness

Timeline

100 BCE   Julius Caesar is born on July 12

85   Caesar's father dies

84   Caesar marries his first wife, Cornelia

82   Sulla takes power in Rome. Caesar refuses to divorce his wife (daughter of one of Sulla's enemies) and has to leave the city and join the army.

79   Sulla dies, and Caesar is able to return to Rome

75   Caesar is captured by pirates on a journey to Rhodes

74   Caesar becomes a war hero after a successful war against Mithradates of Pontus

69   Cornelia dies, and Caesar holds a lavish public funeral. He becomes quaestor, the first step on the Roman political ladder.

67   Caesar marries Pompeia

62   Mounting debts and a scandal surrounding his wife lead Caesar to divorce his wife and leave Rome

61   Caesar becomes governor in Spain, where he conquers new lands and makes himself very rich

59	Caesar becomes consul for the first time, one of the top jobs in Rome. He forms a triumvirate with Pompey and Crassus.
58–50	Caesar's conquest of Gaul
55	Roman forces under Caesar visit Britain for the first time. They will return in 54 BCE.
52	Revolt led by Vercingetorix gives Caesar his greatest challenge in Gaul
49	(January) Caesar marches his army across the Rubicon River, beginning a civil war between Caesar and the forces of the Senate, led by Pompey
48	(August 9) Caesar wins a decisive victory over Pompey at the Battle of Pharsalus. He follows Pompey to Egypt, where Pompey is killed.
46	Caesar defeats his enemies at the Battle of Thapsus in North Africa
44	Caesar is declared dictator of Rome for life
	(March 15) Caesar is murdered on his way to the Senate
27	After many years of war following Caesar's death, his nephew Octavian becomes Rome's first emperor and is known as Augustus

Write Your Own Journal

In addition to being a general and politician, Julius Caesar was also a writer. He wrote many books in his campaigns, which usually showed him in a positive light. For Caesar, they were a great way to advertise his successes.

You probably have different plans for your own journal. It can be a lot of fun to read about your thoughts and feelings a few years later. A public journal or blog lets you explain your views and ideas to other people. Here are some tips on keeping a journal.

- **Who's going to read it?** Before you start, is the journal just for yourself, or do you want others to read it? The words you use and the things you write may be very different depending on what you choose.

- **Where will you write your journal?** You may want to write by hand in a notebook or type your journal on a computer. If you want to share your journal, there are many web sites where you can set up a blog. If you choose this, be careful to stay safe online and never give out personal information about yourself or other people to strangers. This includes your real name, age, address, and the school you go to.

- **What else can you include?** You may just want to include words in the journal, but there are lots of other things you can include, such as photos, letters, e-mails, or links to web sites if you are working online. You may even want to include video or audio recordings. If you are including e-mails from other people or photos showing them in a blog or public journal, you should always check with them first.

- **You could also record a video journal.** Even if you do this, you still need to think about things like your audience and the words you use to express yourself. Make some notes beforehand so you know what you are going to say and make your video diary easy to follow.

- **Make sure you keep writing your journal**. Lots of people start a diary at the beginning of the year and stop after a few days or weeks. Set aside a time each day when you write your journal. Have some question that you ask yourself every time you write to help you get ideas for journal entries, such as:

  - What were the best and worst things that happened today?

  - What was happening in the world today, such as news stories that had an impact on you?

  - If you were reading this journal 100 years from now, what would you want to know about?

Glossary

aedile official in the Roman Republic responsible for maintaining roads and public buildings and for organizing public festivals

ambition goal or success that someone wants to achieve

aristocracy government by a few wealthy or important people, excluding the rest of the people

assassin person who murders someone deliberately, often for political reasons

barbarian for the Romans, anyone who was not Roman was thought to be less cultured and civilized than Romans

bias favoring one point of view or side of an argument

civil war war between two sides from the same country over who will govern the country

consul most important official of the Roman Republic. There were usually two consuls who held the job for a year.

crucify execute someone by hanging him or her from a cross

debt money owed to another person or a bank

dictator single ruler who has sole control over making laws. In the Roman Republic, dictators were normally limited to ruling for a fixed period of time.

empire lands controlled or governed from a foreign country

Gaul region north and west of Rome, which included what is now northern Italy, France, Belgium, and parts of Germany

legion unit of the Roman army

magistrate one of the officials of the Roman Republic, from quaestors to the consuls

praetor senior magistrates who acted as judges and as deputies for the consuls

province part of the Roman Empire outside Italy

quaestor junior magistrate in the Roman Republic

republic state without a king or queen. The Roman Republic ended shortly after Caesar's death, when Octavian became the first Roman emperor.

Senate organization made up of leaders of Rome's oldest and most important families whose role was to advise the magistrates

senator member of the Senate

slave person owned by someone else, who could be bought and sold. Slaves did much of the work in ancient Rome, and some could become rich and powerful.

Find Out More

Books

Bowen, Carl. *Shakespeare's Julius Caesar* (Shakespeare Graphics). Mankato, Minn.: Stone Arch, 2012.

Firth, Rachel. *Julius Caesar* (Young Reading). Tulsa, Okla.: EDC, 2007.

Malam, John. *Ancient Rome* (Time Travel Guides). Chicago: Raintree, 2008.

Middleton, Haydn. *Cleopatra* (True Lives). New York: Oxford University Press, 2009.

Sims, Lesley. *The Roman Soldier's Handbook.* Tulsa, Okla.: EDC, 2005.

Web sites

www.history.com/topics/julius-caesar
Find out more about Julius Caesar on this web site, which includes links to articles on related topics such as ancient Rome and Cleopatra.

www.livius.org/caa-can/caesar/caesar00.html
Learn more about Caesar's life on this web site.

www.socialstudiesforkids.com/articles/worldhistory/ juliuscaesar1.htm
This Social Studies for Kids web site has a biography of Caesar.

Places to visit

There are many Roman remains across Europe and North Africa as well as museums around the world that contain Roman artifacts. Recommended places to visit include:

Rome, Italy: Roman Forum, Colosseum, Baths of Caracalla, and many other remains of the streets that Caesar walked.

Great Britain: Amazing Roman sites include Hadrian's Wall and the museum at Vindolanda, Roman baths at Bath, and the Roman fort at Caerleon, Wales. Roman remains can be seen in many parts of the country.

France: Roman amphitheaters at Arles (city founded by Caesar) and Orange, as well as the magnificent aqueduct of the Pont du Gard.

Topics for further research

- The Roman army: Find out what made this awesome fighting force so successful. What tactics did they use to defeat their enemies?

- Roman culture: What was going in the culture of ancient Rome at this time? Who were some important figures in culture and learning?

- Julius Caesar is one of the most famous Romans, but he was never emperor. Who were the emperors who followed him, and what did they achieve? Who were the best and worst Roman emperors?

Index